Farnborough Technical College
Farnborough
1986

HAMPSHIRE ARCHITECTURE

(1 9 7 4 - 1 9 8 4)

ACADEMY EDITIONS · LONDON | ST. MARTIN'S PRESS · NEW YORK

Hampshire County Council supported the
publication of this book as part of the
1984 Festival of Architecture

Front Cover Drawing by David J. Morriss

First published in 1985 in Great Britain by
Academy Editions 7/8 Holland Street London W8

Copyright © 1985 Hampshire County Council

Published in the United States of America in 1985 by
St. Martin's Press 175 Fifth Avenue New York NY 10010

ISBN 0 312 35730 3 (paper USA only)
ISBN 0 312 35729 X (cloth USA only)

Designed by David J. Morriss

Printed and bound in Hong Kong

CONTENTS

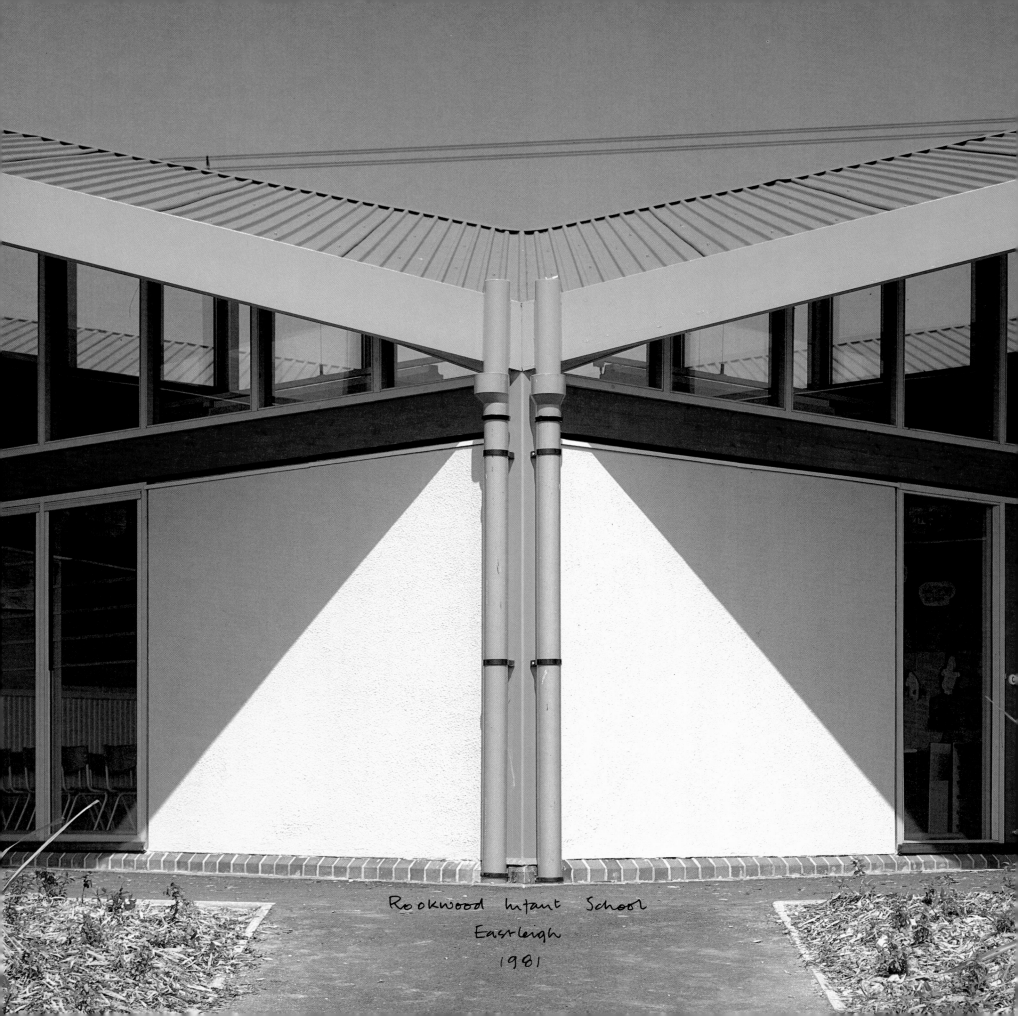

Rookwood Infant School
Eastleigh
1981

Earlier this century local authority buildings were synonymous with a caring human architecture: Arts and Crafts fire stations, L.C.C. housing, cottage hospitals and proud town halls all spoke of creative groups of architects who must have taken great pleasure in how their buildings looked and how they benefited the people they served. In the post second world war era, the multi-disciplinary teamwork and system-build doctrine of Gropius and others was seen as placing architecture on a par with mass production methods, be it sausage, car or tin can factory, and the results invariably gave little comfort to the users or aesthetic pleasure to anyone who observed them. So inevitably wedded became this association of these boring buildings with large corporations and local authorities and other governmental bodies that the earlier achievements of local government are often forgotten.

At the end of the century, now that modernism has lost its influence, it is being demonstrated by several local authorities and new towns that there is a new feeling about architecture in those very organisations where stereotyped teamwork once prevailed. In our 'Post-Modernist' age, given a new approach and attitude not only to architecture but to group working and leadership, it is now possible for individual architects to express creativity and indeed joy in their work. In this atmosphere, enlightened architectural departments are showing — and none is doing this more convincingly than Hampshire — that acts of corporate endeavour can be given positive identity through the skill and craftsmanship of their architects and their care for building users.

Cutting problems down to size is the first step in humanising architecture, and this can be done primarily by restating them. Architects and politicians grossly overstated the problems that faced us in the 50s and 60s, leading to an exaggerated anxiety about the future — particularly in coping with imaginary effects of rapid change, shortage in the building stock and the impact of new technology. Heroic grand plans, major demolition and rebuilding programmes, and a reliance on utopian philosophies were all seen as appropriate responses to the desperate plights it was imagined were about to befall us. In time, a much calmer and more realistic and appropriate role for architecture has been identified, which has gone hand in hand with re-learning how to make simpler buildings that are truly part of everyday living and not merely the by-products of socially revolutionary forces. In this mood, real needs can be much more easily identified and one in particular that has emerged is that the quality of human life must be closely related to the quality of the environment that society creates for itself. The continued success of counties like Hampshire lies in the value put on protecting existing attractive countryside, as well as valuing an architectural heritage which was not ruined by 19th and early 20th century industrial development. Future economic growth in particular has become increasingly identified with capitalising on good environments (good places to be in). Today's newer industries, particularly the knowledge-based ones, can choose whatever location they want, being freed of dependence on mineral extraction or transport networks or labour pools in the conventional sense. The success of such new buildings that are required, be it for work, home or leisure, can now be seen as directly related to the importance given to broad based environmental issues at the outset. In this climate, a county that invests in the kind of architectural environment Hampshire is doing must succeed at many levels.

As we enter an era of low or no growth, conservationism has quite rightly become a central social issue. It is probably not generally known that Hampshire spends more on conservation than any other county. The County Architect's Department is, of course, very directly involved in this sphere, with projects like Fort Nelson, Basing House, Winchester Great Hall, Odiham Castle, Bursledon Windmill and a mass of Victorian village primary schools built in a range of materials including knapped flint, stone, brick, tile and slate. In this day and age, one can't begin to ape the skills demonstrated in the earlier centuries: indeed architects and public opinion have recognised the pleasures that can be got from enjoying past artistry and workmanship, and that modern skills and technology are often better employed in keeping the best of the past rather than demolishing it.

Finally, an architecture which responds to individuals and respects identity demands unusual organisational and leadership attitudes; it is much easier to lead a so-called 'team' when all its members are subordinates to preconceived methods and solutions. It is much more worthwhile but more difficult to bring out a wider creative contribution from individual architects who respond to different opportunities in different ways, and to utilise a much wider palette of colour, technology and spatial construction. The success of Hampshire's Architects Department is due not only to changed architectural attitudes and philosophies but also to mastering these new teamwork skills.

The primary task of our time is to humanise the social, industrial and technological advances of the past 200 years whilst coping with the increasing depersonalisation and loss of identity within our society due to population expansion, growth of massive organisations and authorities, and modern communications. The work shown in this book demonstrates that a department within a large local government authority can build a human architecture and, I believe, that good architecture today, and its approval by the public, is possible.

Terry Farrell

Fort Hill Community School
Basingstoke
1978

Red House Health Centre
Eastleigh
1980

Through the grey light of these conservative times, one perceives the spread of a hopeless doctrine: a new version of a doctrine that is as old as authoritarianism: a doctrine that would have us believe that the client for a building is only he who pays for it, he with the power: a doctrine that is almost certain to lead us further towards an architecture that is enclosed and separated from the world without, stodgy, box-like and finite, zoned, roomed and corridored, and elevated symmetrically, pompously and in a revivalistic way in order to establish each building's separate status. In the conservative frame of mind, the tendency to accept the location of money and power as an indicator of what to do is often called 'being realistic', as though money and power were more real than the actual and latent power of the rest of the people, more real than our inter-relationships across the surface of the globe and through the communities and cities that we have made on it, and more real than our attempts to live together in some harmony, and in peace, in weather and climate, under the sun.

Now it must be said that this wonderfully uninspiring doctrine is at least in part a reaction to the post-war period, during which it was thought that a beneficent state could provide for the needs of the people, through its own bureaucracy, and by employing architects to take responsibility for 'getting it right' without the reactive benefit of talking directly to the future users of the buildings. Increasingly the state tried to do this by establishing an enormous number of guidelines, procedures and planning and building systems that had the effect of partially removing the creative egos of architects from the mix as well. And it is in counteracting this last, the deadly effects of standardisation and the depression of designers' egos, that I think that Hampshire have largely succeeded. They have certainly achieved a studio-like atmosphere in a local authority office, an atmosphere in which individual and group creative expression can thrive. Can thrive to make particular, sometimes elegant, sometimes witty, always unsystemised, colourful buildings that respond to the situations in which they are found and which, in a more general sense, are a positive response to popular desires and popular pressure.

Maybe it goes without saying that it needs a responsive, expressive architecture to respond to popular pressure, for only with a rich and versatile vocabulary can one respond at all. During the 40s, 50s and early 60s, therefore, the old ministry-approved house and system-built flats and schools could respond formally to little more than a demand for newness.

They were certain to falter in the 70s and now in the 80s when people, disappointed by the blandness, sameness and shabbiness of systems, are energetically demanding a say in the feel of things. Naturally, the disappointment results partly in nostalgia for past times and old-fashioned architecture, but it seems to me that to revive old styles is to deny all of us, architects and customers alike, the joy and stimulus of invention and creation. As William Morris said in his 1889 address to the Society for the Protection of Ancient Buildings:

"It cannot be, it has gone! They believe that we can do the same sort of work in the same spirit as our forefathers, whereas for good and for evil we are completely changed, and we cannot do the work they did. All continuity of history means is after all perpetual change, and it is not hard to see that we have changed with a vengeance, and thereby established our claim to be the continuers of history."

So knowing as I do of the lengths to which one must go today to talk to and respond to the feelings of the users of buildings, and knowing of the hundreds of conversations the Hampshire architects have, I am thankful that they do so with an architecture that is expressive and responsive enough to make that process into a genuine one; an architecture that contains choices in its essence, an architecture that has style, an architecture about which it is possible to have conversations, and an architecture that has at least the commitment of the egos of the individuals and groups who design it. For without that, how could it be architecture?

Currently there is a debate, often more like a mud-slinging contest, in which all recent buildings are described as 'modern architecture'. If they must be called architecture, which is to vastly devalue the word, then the towers and slabs and boxes that surround us can only represent a low level version of that branch or part of modernism which supports standardisation, factory assembly, repetition and with it a reductivist aesthetic and an object like quality for buildings. At the same time, this way of thought supports industrialisation and therefore the devaluing of craftsmanship. There is however another, far nobler, tradition within the modern movement; a tradition that might be represented by the work of Mackintosh, the prairie houses of Frank Lloyd Wright, the Schröder House, Ronchamp and the Stuttgart Gallery; a tradition that sees architecture as contributing to a society that seeks to be liberated and less formal in its relationships.

Hatch Warren Primary School
Basingstoke
1984

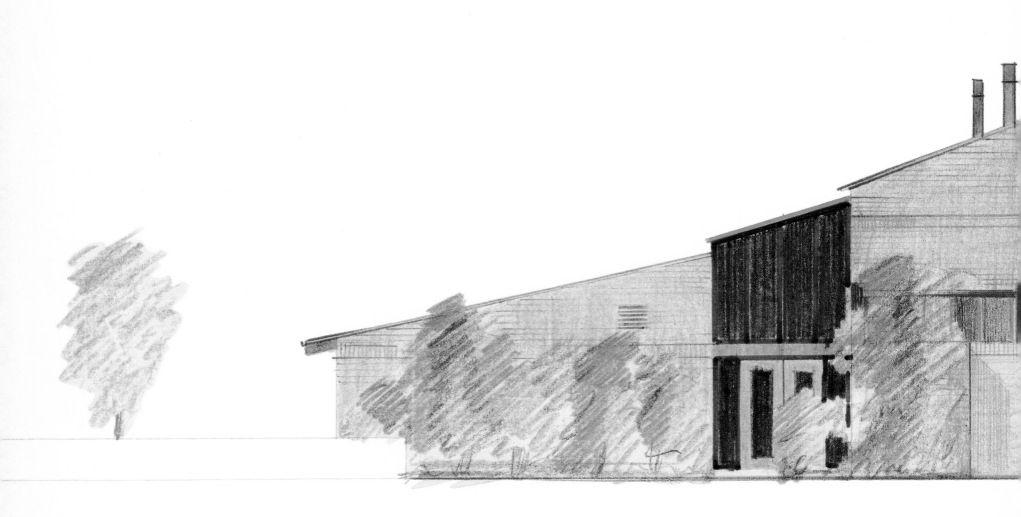

Burnham Copse Infant School
Tadley
1985

It was always proposed to assist this progress by understanding architecture in the cubist tradition as the composition of routes and paths and places, asymmetrically, as partly enclosed, partly open space; coloured and lit by the sun to reveal form and effect. It is also an architecture that is humanist and sensual and sensitive to our needs for privacy and being together, to our needs for degrees of contact, by using the design of space to achieve it rather than by the old 'rooms off corridors' method of planning. It is a hopeful way of thinking and composing that still has great distances to run, developing to become more delicate, particular and responsive. This is the tradition to which the Hampshire architects are connected; the tradition that Aldo Van Eyck refers to when he talks about the 'Great Gang' of optimistic, inventive, logical humanists who changed our understanding of the world and its possibilities forever, early in this century.

If the opposite to finite, enclosed and status-ridden architecture can be described as that which welcomes the interpretation of public and private places, which makes welcoming, calmly ordered buildings that are carefully considered in the three formal dimensions and in the fourth dimension of use, that respond to their sites and their neighbours and are detailed to celebrate their making; then one must say that the buildings of Hampshire have made a significant local contribution to this way of thought and source of inspiration. They are securely and energetically in the hopeful tradition of architecture which is known in Europe as 'open form'.

Edward Cullinan

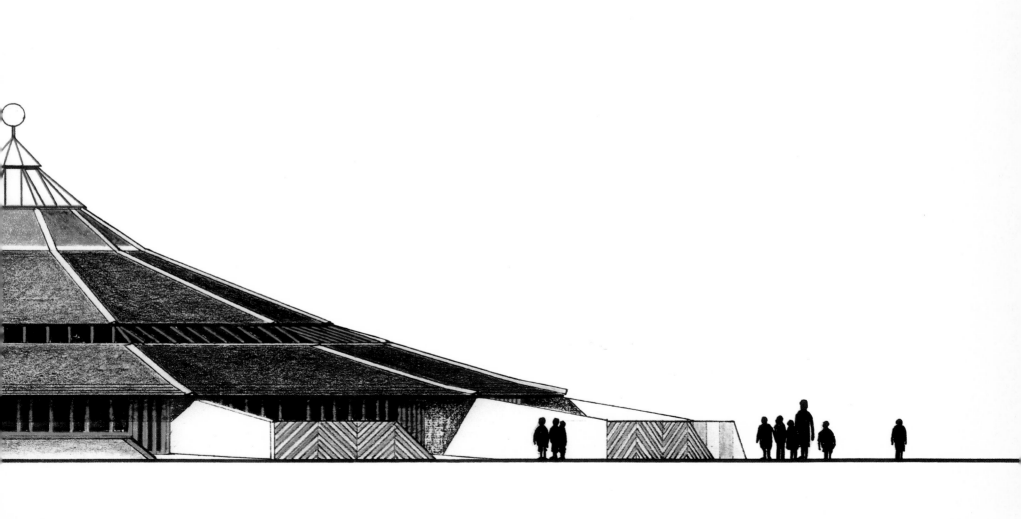

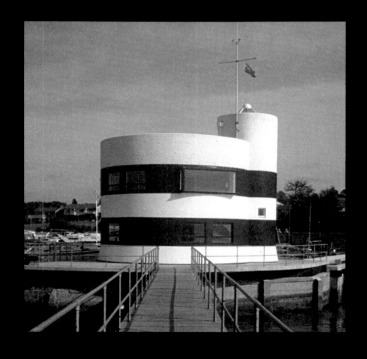

River Hamble Harbour Masters Office,

Warsash

1978

Four Lanes Primary School
Chineham
1982

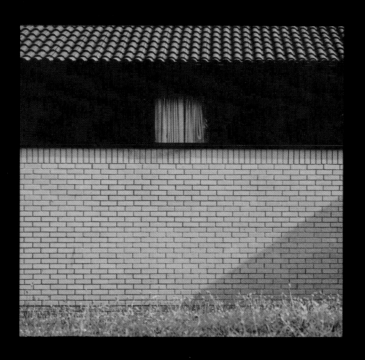

St Francis Special School
Fareham
1978

Newlands Primary School
Yateley
1979

RICHARD MACCORMAC

Good architecture is rare. So to find a county in which the public architecture ranges from the good to the exceptional is rather like coming across a nature reserve which nurtures some remarkable species. You react with surprise and pleasure, and wonder about the conditions which encouraged this fertility.

For the new buildings of Hampshire, illustrated in this book, present a freshness and plurality of ideas far removed from the uniformity once expected of local authorities. They advocate a creative philosophy, concerned with public good, but quite distinct from what Colin Stansfield Smith refers to as 'that ideal, rational and fair world' envisaged in post-war social policy and ossified in collective standards and prefabricated building systems. This release from uniformity and emergence of intuitive design represents for me an affirmation of freedom and of human values in public architecture and a lifeline for other areas of corporate society, musclebound by bureaucracy.

In the supposedly 'ideal, rational and fair world', design was prescribed in the measurable terms of area, cost and 'environmental performance'. The awkward and untidy insights of personal opinion were erased because they were unaccountable and supposedly compromised objectives. Everywhere today we can see, in retrospect, the failure of that frame of mind, the road engineering that destroyed historic places, the mass-produced housing unrelated to personal aspirations, and the schools built in the meaningless image of constructional convenience.

The architecture of Hampshire is part of a return to the primacy of architecture itself, and to the belief, unreconciled in the theories of the modern movement, that expressive intentions need not compromise the way a building works, but may extend and transform the very idea of what a building is and what it is for.

An example is the powerful theme of glazed roofs which has been developed in the new Hampshire schools, and gives them their distinct character. Delightful effects of light and volume, so dramatically evident in schools such as Bosmere, have arisen from explorations of conservatory-like spaces with gains in floor area and savings in energy. At Crestwood School, the development of this theme has produced a glazed street which gives a new dimension to school life, a forum for the school community, and a public place for weddings and festivals. Through this architectural transformation, the idea of 'school' is itself transformed and its social purpose extended.

Throughout the county, architecture is being created with constructional elegance, ranging from the use of traditional materials in housing and health centres to high technology for more complex long span structures such as Boyatt Hostel for the Physically Handicapped. Most characteristic is what Colin Stansfield Smith likes to call 'the bicycle chain aesthetic', the eclectic assembly of appropriate materials and parts — timber, steel and glass, with a lack of aesthetic prejudice which enables the buildings to be made in the most pertinent way. There is no corporate image, but no lack of style either; the architectural themes are the styles — big barns, glazed roofs and the Utzon-like projects with asymmetrical metal roofs floating above massed brickwork.

What unites these projects is a commitment to quality in the intrinsic sense, not as a decorative addition in the Post-Modernist sense. At Chandlers Ford Library, the branching timber structure makes a cloister-like grove. Perhaps archaic memories are stirred: such is the quality of the place.

So how does all this come about? Colin Stansfield Smith speaks of his concern for product, not process — a commitment which I believe distinguishes all good architectural practice. For the product must be the motivating force. In Hampshire, this is manifest in the architectural themes which galvanise the office, its 'in-house eclecticism', complemented from time to time by the work of outside consultants: Ahrends Burton and Koralek, Aldington Craig and Collinge, and Ted Cullinan amongst them.

It is a characteristic of the office that senior architects (including the chief) stay on the drawing boards, resisting the temptation to back off the critical challenge of design for the bureaucratic demands of paper work. For to me there is no doubt that part of the failure of post-war British architecture is attributable to the retreat of experienced architects from the front line of design: good design is an accumulation of experience, sensitivity and insight.

Finally, this work depends upon the elected Members of the County Council who have had the confidence to sustain and patronise architecture as of higher value itself. This is an important and continuing act of faith. For society really does get the architecture it asks for, if not the architecture it deserves.

Richard MacCormac

Elson Infant School
Gosport
1984

Crestwood School & Community Centre
Eastleigh

Hostel for the Younger Physically Disabled
Eastleigh
1985

Ringwood Sports Centre
Ringwood
1982

Hulbert Middle School

Waterlooville

1982

library & Health Centre Porchester
Jackson Greenen & Down & Partners
1984

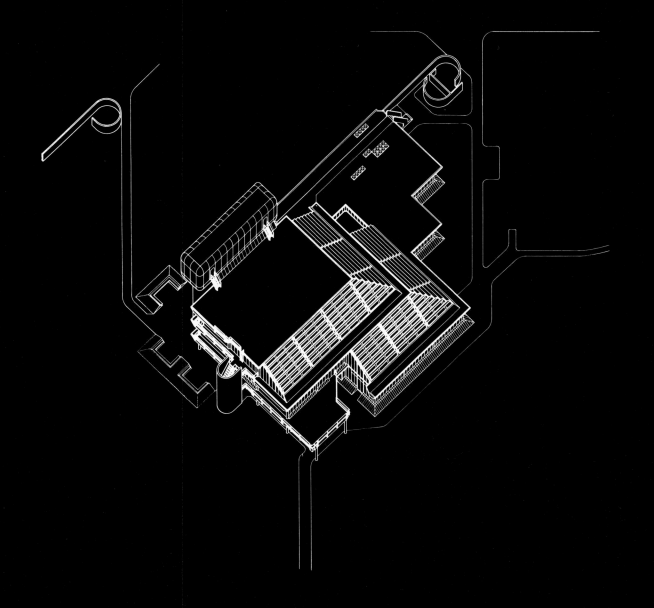

Portsmouth Polytechnic Library

Ahrends Burton & Koralek

1979

D. Day Museum

Portsmouth City Architects Department

1984

Southampton Hall of Aviation

Southampton City Architects Department

1984

Special School & Hostel project Basingstoke
Aldington Craig & Collinge
1985

Calthorpe Park Secondary School Refurbishment Fleet
Edward Cullinan Architects
1984

Velmead Junior School Project Fleet
Michael Hopkins Architects
1986

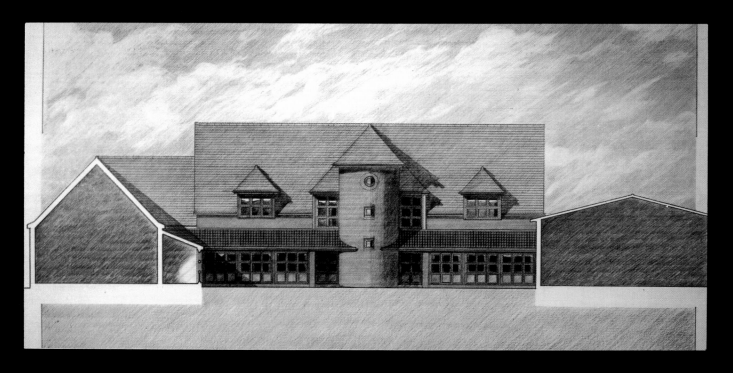

Tower Hill Primary School Extensions Cove
Robert Adam / Evans Roberts & Partners
1985

NEW LIBRARY · BORDON · HAMPSHIRE

MCMLXXXIIII

METRES

EVANS ROBERTS & PARTNERS

FOR THE COUNTY ARCHITECT

ROBERT ADAM

Local authority building is by definition for the common good: clearly most architecture is not.

However, both private and public clients are presumably capable of comparing the benefits of building with benefits achieved by other means. Therefore it might be argued that one of the duties of local authority architects is to make clear — if not emphasise — the particular contribution that their buildings make to social and community activities, both those in being and those considered desirable.

Such architectural emphasis can justifiably be regarded as necessary for increasing both the providers' and the users' quality of perception and comparison. A similar case can scarcely be made out for the private sector.

All architecture should contribute beyond its functional intent. The private sector by its nature, even when offering a service, tends to be exclusive and its buildings act as fortresses, with curtain walls on the boundaries. The same concept governed local authority planning until recently, with chain link fencing protecting bland anonymous buildings from the public who express their resentment by vandalism. Now, at last, we are beginning to see in our public buildings the reflection of a new attitude of participation, which encourages in the community a sense of pride in its involvement and shared ownership. The intention of these buildings is to celebrate, by the variety of their form and colour, a new confidence and purpose based on public support and approval.

Whereas local authorities have statutory obligations to provide certain services requiring buildings, the private sector is primarily motivated by commercial interests. On the surface it might seem that the latter would be more flexible in equating the built form to alternative action and expenditure. There is therefore a greater onus on the part of local authorities to anticipate rather than respond to future beneficial social mores and patterns. Whilst the intent, and indeed content, of most local authority building is admirable, it has tended to favour the ponderous and austere in form rather than the elegant or delightful. The worthiness of the aims of local authority building is not questioned here: rather, whether those who initiate — not design — such undertakings are aware of the rapid increase of available alternatives to some of the services which frequently require little or no architectural input.

But who within the local authority should beg the question about the built solutions, particularly some of the institutional ones? Domiciliary care is now frequently preferred by social services. Even so, institutions are still being promulgated, and the quality of the brief too often influences the quality of the building for better or worse.

In the main, local authorities prefer the conventional answer — built or otherwise. You are right to suggest that local authorities have a duty to be conscious of innovation, because by their nature they are hidebound by the answer that has gone before and found universal acceptance. These answers tend to be self-perpetuating, rather like the bureaucracy that supports and nurtures them. The design stereotype is ever present.

There remains today in the strategy of local authority planning an assumption of long term growth. A building project first appears at the far end of a five year programme and, as time passes, the political pressure for its realisation increases, with too little consideration as to its continuing validity.

The massive programme for national literacy initiated in the nineteenth century, though retarded by the two world wars, was given enormous impetus by the 1944 Education Act. This impetus was not merely echoed but enriched by the massive schools building programme in the post-1945 years. Space, colour, light and scale responsive to children became the norm and, in all probability, increased the attraction of joining the teaching profession.

Architecture is seldom viewed as a generator of a new and better quality of life for those who inhabit it. This role should not be ignored. Neither should the fact that good architecture can increase the aspirations of those who use it, and in so doing increase its own rate of obsolescence.

In a period of cash limited building maintenance funds, the construction of new buildings actually threatens the survival of the existing building stock. Demolition has itself become a creative act, breaking the self-perpetuation of obsolete, decaying buildings of the 50s and 60s and releasing funds for the rejuvenation of a smaller, more intensively used, public estate.

Now, in public buildings such as schools, civic theatres and community centres, the continuous pressures for improvement of both the structures and the services they provide have, since the 40s, been met by the renewal of the existing, or replacement by similar building types.

Crestwood School & Community Centre
Eastleigh
1982

Henry Cort School Sports Hall
Fareham
1982

Four Lanes Primary School
Chineham
1982

However, dissimilar alternatives are proving increasingly efficacious. The home-based computer is more often the property of the children than of the parents. The home video library is serviced by video tape shops (which now outnumber bookshops in Britain) rather than the public library. Few local action groups meet in the Town Hall, private bus companies shun the civic depot, whilst community work replaces prison sentences. Similar changes are of course taking place in the private and commercial sector of the built environment, but in most cases the value and quality of the redundant structures encourages not only replacement but resiting both here and overseas. Oxford Street is depopulating rapidly, whilst more and more 'British' cars are made abroad.

In this context, it is extremely interesting to view the current and recent works by the architects acting for Hampshire County Council. In a very large county with a varied range of population growth areas it is not surprising to find a predominance of educational buildings. What is surprising is the similarities and the peculiarities of such buildings.

Considering the similarities, I am struck by the extraordinary preoccupation with roofs. These roofs are not merely required to shelter and enclose, but are used to signal the variety of volumes they cover, to indicate the nature of contained uses, to emphasise complexity, to unify the simple and to provide long range identity and colour. A variety of structures, materials, forms and colours are employed to this end, making the roof the School Cap and Blazer for the inevitably similar being contained within.

It is as if compulsory education were a new and questionable benefit that required this colourfully sculptured identification. Could it also indicate a desire on the part of the designer to establish a visual focus if not dominance in a sea of indifferent domestic building and bland, flat landscape?

For too long the space around school buildings has expressed a narrow view of its function solely to provide for sport and physical exercise. The educational and social potential of a controlled landscape with trees and shrubs providing shelter, enclosure, and a habitat for wild life is only now starting to be realised.

Such a landscape is worth mentioning since so many of the buildings appear on generous sites where the resultant single or two storey form compensates for its own flattened shape with the sculptured external

The peculiarities or individual identities of the buildings are expressed internally more in form than materials. With one or two exceptions, the materials, their assembly, juxtaposition and finishing are all rather friendly, giving the impression that a benevolent, very superior do-it-yourself firm was involved. This conscious openness or clarity of form and finish can be mistaken for naïveté in some instances, where the sheer delight in geometric complexity seems more to do with clever puzzles than with the gentle subtlety of assembling an environment for learning. However, here and there the imagination of fearless professionalism breaks through. Here, an apparently formless school draws its strength from a balconied street, which stretches both the pedagogic mind and pupil awareness. There, a debilitated, anaemic bit of town street, with its inevitable hidden, worn out fringes is reordered and revitalised with an extraordinary column-forested half doughnut of a library.

By designing spaces which uplift the user through their celebratory character, the architect enables functions to develop never dreamed of in the brief. The right building erected in the right place at the right time, in addition to fulfilling its own function, can transform local values, and encourage the redevelopment of a surrounding run down area. The creation of a community school will not of itself provide an effective focus for community activities unless the users perceive a unique sense of place in the welcoming but protective enclosure of the buildings and the spaces between them.

Hampshire has always been a county of contrasts — the few vast estates, the few very big cities, and the gigantic tracts of in-between land — with trees, asbestos cement tiles, horses, filling stations, big roads and shallow ditches, empty churches and maintenance depots, tired villages and directionless suburbs, dark porches and distant views.

Both ponies and punks can feel at ease with this extraordinarily heartening range of new architecture. Its attitude to posterity is admirably ambivalent, which architecture must be if it is to enrich change with the accumulated wisdom of the present. Style it has, and it puts humanity back into fashion.

Observations by Cedric Price
with interjections by the County Architect

COLIN STANSFIELD SMITH

The skills of the talented designer architect should now be at a premium in public service — but there is little evidence that they are. Extolling the virtues of estate management, no matter how necessary, is hardly likely to attract these skills into the fold. Managing a large public estate with its inherent responsibilities of an historic heritage, making it more efficient in energy and running costs, adjusting, re-organising and rationalising it, maintaining it and at times demolishing the redundant parts of it; all these are activities which are a necessary part of a design centre but are subsumed in it.

The vision and enterprise, even the entrepreneurial skill required for estate management depends on the quality and emphasis given to design. Good design must be 'up front' to popularise the whole idea of building. It cannot be something that is taken for granted. Much more, it needs to be the visible shop window of an enlightened local authority, something that it can take pride in and perhaps in its more confident moments even boast about. It should infiltrate the visual standards of everything from signwriting and graphics to interior design, and a good deal in between. It should not be restricted to buildings, but should include spaces and environments generally, involving at the same time collaboration with artists and sculptors.

Architects are the rightful custodians of the public estate because they have the capacity to introduce joy, imagination and wit into our environments. It is not merely a question of creating a climate in which excellence in architecture and the collaborative arts can be achieved (this would be virtuous and commendable but is so often only a token gesture in reality); a public authority must itself be creative to the point where what it does is an inspiration for others.

Public architects in the last ten years have had to operate at an increasingly complex, difficult and sometimes hostile interface with their public. Dealing in the 70s and 80s with existing buildings rather than just with new ones they have had to satisfy the needs of building users as well as administrative and adviser clients. This is in contrast with the 60s, when new buildings on green field sites were provided in advance of the appointment of users (such as headmasters and college principals). This ongoing relationship with the users of buildings presents the public architect with a whole series of opportunities, all with a public relations commitment. In 1985, a large proportion of the public estate alienates rather than celebrates the very purpose it was originally built to serve and much of this alienated estate was conceived

during the last forty years. Many of its associations and images are depressingly institutional, box-like, corridored, uniform and drab — frequently bounded by that nadir for all public estates, the concrete post and chain link fence. This depressing environment can and must be changed if there is any justification for having architects 'in house'.

Although it is difficult to engender a feeling of confidence and optimism in these stringent times, extensions to existing buildings should still be seen as an opportunity to improve whole environments rather than as the execution of some new efficiency game. Building is not just a ruinous expense, informed only by impersonal facts and figures and objective scientific method. Credibility for the designer now attaches to the individual not the profession, to the identity of the individual site and the calibre of the particular design team. Individuality deserves recognition.

Architecture should be put back into its proper place as an art, with its essence acknowledged as a valid intention in building. This would liberalise attitudes to architecture. It could promote a relationship between a public architect and the users of the buildings for which he is responsible, similar to a musician and his audience. Architecture is essentially about celebration: its business, apart from performing its basic function, is to make life pleasurable and to enhance its meaning.

But the contemporary concern appears not to be about quality but about efficiency: about more and more numbers and more and more measurement. Any institution the size of local government finds it difficult to accommodate individuality — matters of opinion, matters of taste; it succumbs to collective, objective consistency to the point where the design stereotype is almost impossible to avoid, from the impact of guidelines, bulletins and endless prescription. To attempt to personalise would involve accusations of 'ego trip', self-centred indulgence, elitism. Creative skills are difficult to remunerate in a system that only recognises and measures objectively and reveres the status of management to the detriment of professional judgement. To practise architecture calls for considerable skills; to practise architecture well means giving an important part of your mind; to practise architecture extremely well means giving your life. That sort of commitment is required in social architecture. These days it seems difficult enough to make a building happen at all. To realise architecture with some or all of its concomitant associations is to achieve a real bonus.

Colin Stansfield Smith

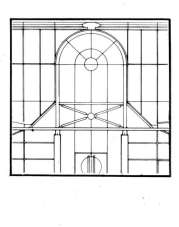
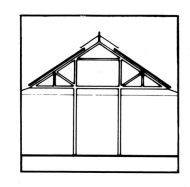
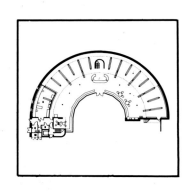
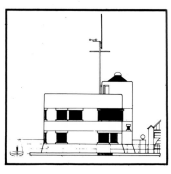
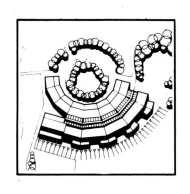
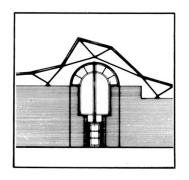
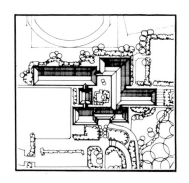
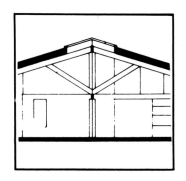
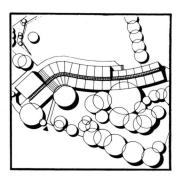

S E L E C T E D   P R O J E C T S

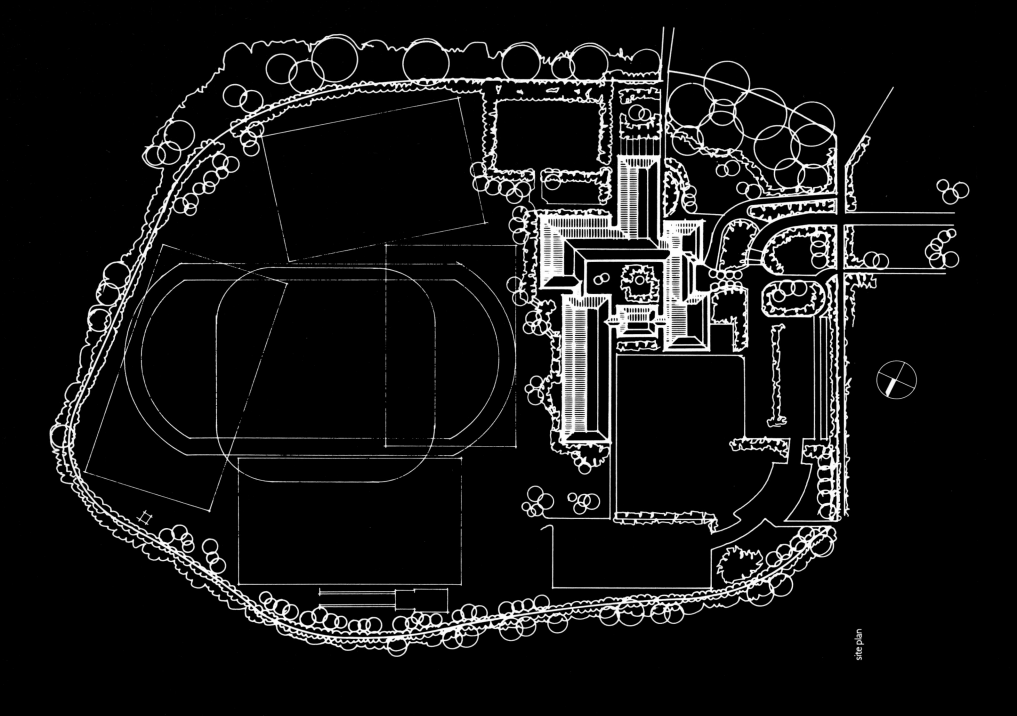

site plan

FORT HILL SCHOOL

This school lies within Winklebury Camp, north of Winklebury Centre, Basingstoke. It is an Iron Age fort, and archaeological excavations were carried out by the Department of the Environment before the start of the building contract. There are slight falls from the centre of the site in all directions, with a substantial hedge on two-thirds of the perimeter. The Iron Age ditch still exists to the south and east, but to the north only a bank remains.

An attempt was made to reduce the building scale, which can often be so daunting in schools of this size, by slightly sinking the mainly single storey buildings into the ground. It is hoped that the highly modelled roof and ridge tiles and the landscaped central court have also helped to bring an oriental flavour to the school.

The construction is an amalgam of school and house building practice, with fairfaced brickwork, a reinforced concrete frame supporting trussed rafters and concrete roof tiles with clay ridge tiles and finials.

ST. FRANCIS SPECIAL SCHOOL

St. Francis Special School lies within a large campus also containing separate schools for juniors, infants and physically disabled children.

A major trunk road to the north, and slopes facing south towards attractive, mature woodland, suggested a building form with protective workshop areas, hall, kitchen, services and staff room facing north, shielding the teaching bases and dining room which share the view to the south. Pedestrian and vehicular entrances are quite separate, though following parallel winding courses to reach the building.

The design provides for eight study bases, ten children in each, leading from shared areas. Each base has its own bay window seat, looking out onto a private terrace for outdoor teaching. The dining room also has its own terrace. The building's staggered plan and the serrated roofline, which gives each unit its pitched roof, achieves a domestic scale.

ST. FRANCIS SPECIAL SCHOOL
KEY

1. BASE
2. HOUSECRAFT
3. BATHROOM
4. GIRLS TOILET
5. BOYS TOILET
6. WORKSHOP
7. SHARED AREA
8. STORE
9. HALL
10. DINING/CIRCULATION
11. KITCHEN
12. CLOAKS
13. BOILERS
14. CARETAKER
15. MALE STAFF TOILET
16. FEMALE STAFF TOILET

17. QUIET ROOM
18. M.I. ROOM
19. SECRETARY
20. HEADMASTER
21. STAFF ROOM
22. TOILETS
23. UTILITY
24. SPLASH
25. MOST SEVERELY
    HANDICAPPED UNIT
26. GARDEN STORE
27. GARDEN
28. TERRACE
29. DINING TERRACE
30. SERVICE AREA
31. M.S.H. GARDEN

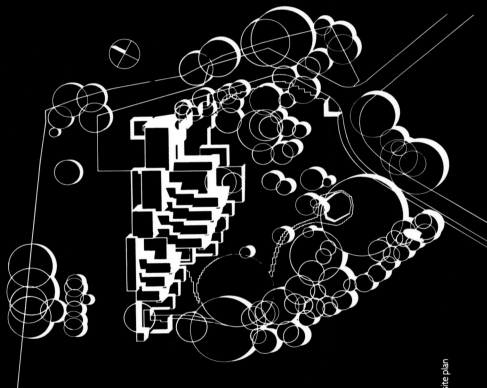

site plan

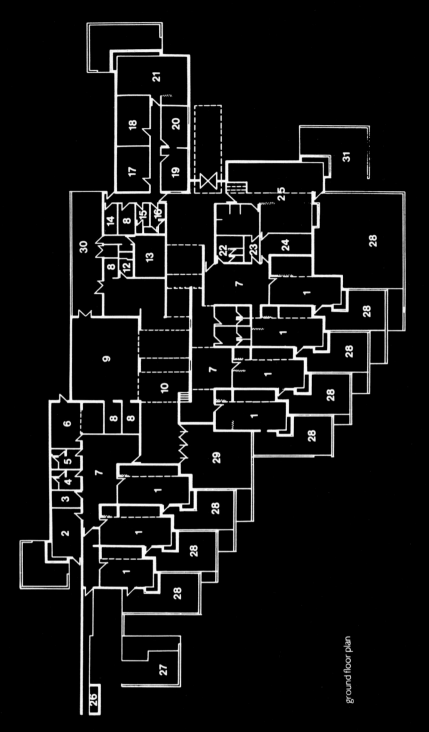

ground floor plan

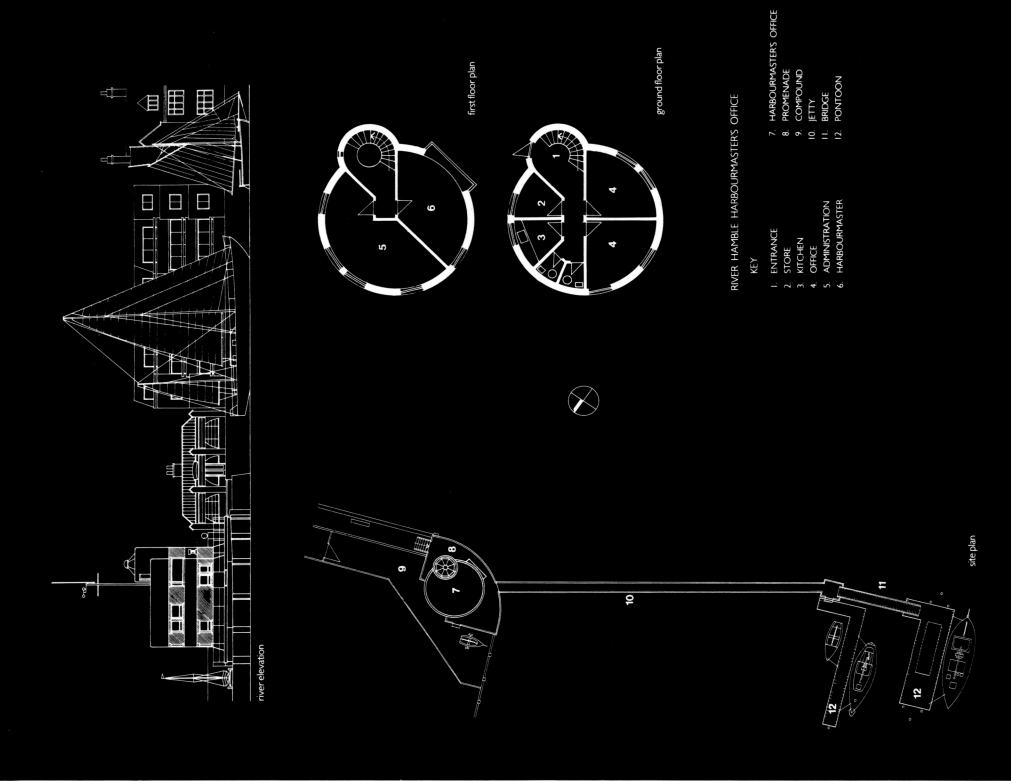

first floor plan

ground floor plan

river elevation

site plan

RIVER HAMBLE HARBOURMASTER'S OFFICE

KEY

1. ENTRANCE
2. STORE
3. KITCHEN
4. OFFICE
5. ADMINISTRATION
6. HARBOURMASTER
7. HARBOURMASTER'S OFFICE
8. PROMENADE
9. COMPOUND
10. JETTY
11. BRIDGE
12. PONTOON

RIVER HAMBLE
HARBOURMASTER'S OFFICE

On the banks of the River Hamble lie many boat-yards and in recent years four large marinas have been established which, together with the County Council's moorings, provide berths for approximately 2,500 vessels in the river estuary. It remains the base of a small but profitable inshore fishery.

The brief called for a layout of floating pontoons, linked to a shore office by a hinged bridge and jetty, with access from a large public car park. Office accommodation was required for the Harbour Master, with mess and storage facilities and toilets. One of the few conditions imposed by the client was that the office should have views both up and down stream.

The District Planning Authority sought, through the development, to obtain a major environmental improvement of the site, which was a semi-derelict eyesore, but began by insisting that any building must be of no more than one storey and of inconspicuous appearance. Nevertheless, in the end it gave its full support to the design of the building, produced in the face of much local opposition.

The building was intended to be nautical in style and to have

"the uncompromising geometry and restricted symbolic colouring of the standard Trinity House buoy ... severe and evocative rather than decorative" (John Piper: 'The Nautical Style', Architectural Review, Jan. 1938).

NEWLANDS PRIMARY SCHOOL

The form of this building attempts to combine the educational benefits of a deep plan layout with a selective approach to environmental control — making use of daylighting, natural ventilation and solar gains.

The brief stressed the qualitative aspects of the educational environment and, in particular, the significance of scale and variety. It also stressed the concept of the teaching cluster, capable of a range of different organisational patterns and catering for age differences, variety in groupings, and individual teaching preferences.

Accommodation is grouped in two distinct blocks: the first contains junior and infant teaching clusters; the second, the hall and music room together with an administration suite, kitchen for 200 meals, and other ancillary accommodation. The central glazed courtyard provides an additional external teaching facility, useful for most of the school year, and allows landscaping to be brought into the heart of the building.

To achieve a gradual transition from the outside, external finishes such as the timber soffit boarding and brick paving continue inside the building. Brick boundary walls are carried into the building to form external walls on the north and east sides.

NEWLANDS PRIMARY SCHOOL

KEY

1. KITCHEN STAFF ROOM
2. PLANT ROOM
3. MEDICAL ROOM
4. OFFICE
5. HEADMASTER'S OFFICE
6. RECEPTION
7. STORE
8. W.C.
9. KITCHEN
10. MUSIC ROOM
11. HALL
12. CONSERVATORY
13. RESOURCE
14. HOME BASE
15. SHARED AREA
16. HOME PLAY
17. CLASSROOM
18. TUTORIAL
19. WET PRACTICAL AREA

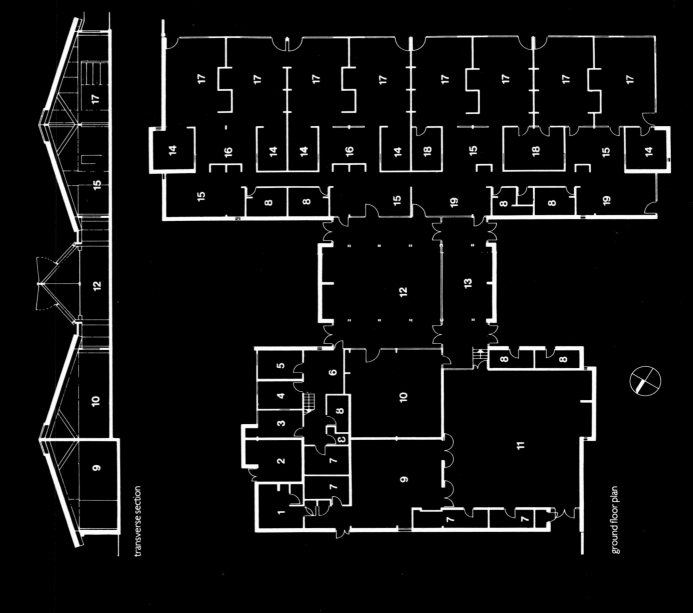

transverse section

ground floor plan

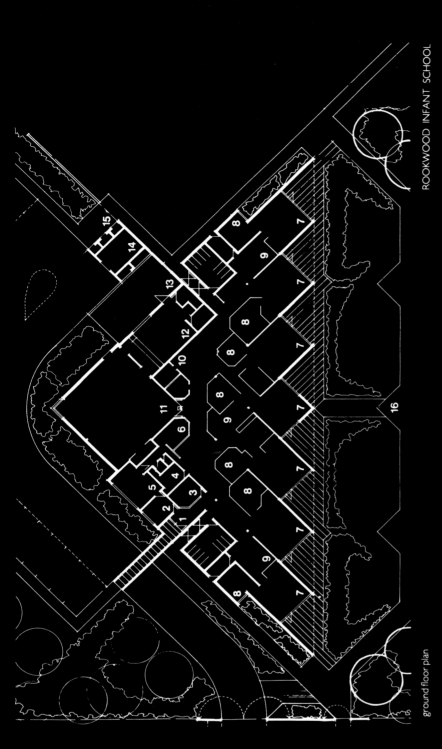

ground floor plan

ROOKWOOD INFANT SCHOOL

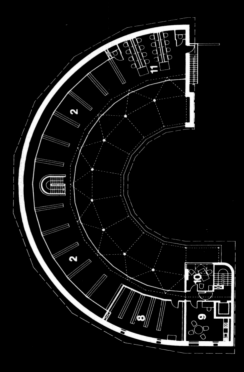

first floor plan

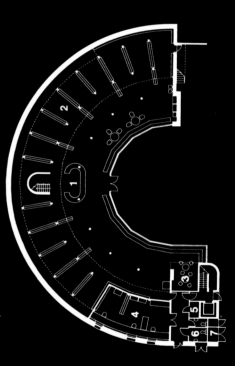

ground floor plan

CHANDLER'S FORD LIBRARY

ROOKWOOD INFANT SCHOOL

This school serves part of a large new estate on the north side of Eastleigh. The rectangular site slopes gently down to the south and lies on the edge of an estate between new and existing housing.

The triangular single storey building is placed near the main access at the north west corner of the site, with the seven classrooms all facing south over the playcourt. Apart from the PE / dining hall, kitchen, and administrative suite, the main teaching areas are designed in an open plan arrangement using furniture and moveable partitions to divide the space.

The timber and steel structural frame supports a series of monopitch roofs incorporating north light windows to provide daylight at the centre of the building. Rendered insulating blockwork alternates with timber framed storey height windows.

The roof covers small verandahs outside each classroom which are thus shielded from excessive solar gain in summer. The building benefits from its southerly aspect to reduce the need for central heating in spring and autumn.

CHANDLER'S FORD LIBRARY

This project combines the provision of a new public library with an attempt to enhance the community focus of the local shopping centre.

The site is a long rectangular strip of backland behind the main thorough-fare with a narrow frontage onto a side road. Facing down a newly created public footpath to the main thoroughfare, the library demonstrates the development potential of the two adjoining areas of land.

The building form, a solid arc with transparent inner curve, embraces a courtyard, drawing people in, sheltering and proclaiming the function. The mural on the inside of the curved rear wall provides a backdrop to the radial pattern of library shelving glimpsed by pedestrians from the courtyard. Vehicular access is from the side road to the building's rear, giving complete separation from pedestrians.

FOUR LANES PRIMARY SCHOOL

KEY

1. RECEPTION
2. HALL
3. CENTRAL AREA
4. CLASSROOM
5. TUTORIAL
6. MUSIC/DRAMA
7. KITCHEN
8. ADMINISTRATION

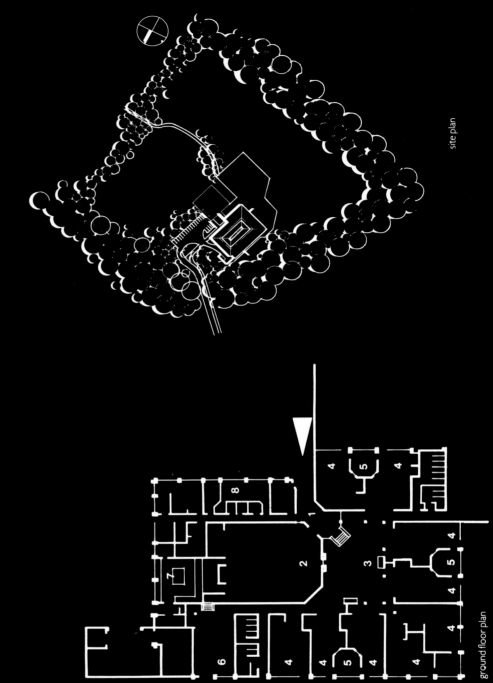

site plan

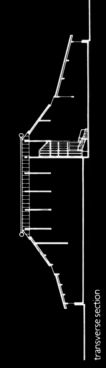

longitudinal section

transverse section

ground floor plan

FOUR LANES PRIMARY SCHOOL

The rear wall encloses a line of tree-like timber columns which together support the pitched roof. The timber branches at high level form a continuous horizontal wind girder braced at each end of the building by brick gables. The first floor, supported independently on piers, is set away from the rear wall enabling the full height of the mural to be lit by daylight from above.

FOUR LANES PRIMARY SCHOOL

This school serves an area of new housing to the north east of Basingstoke, built on undulating arable farmland and woodland.

The building is designed as a junior school with two forms of entry, but will accommodate the full 5-11 primary age range until an infant school is added. Nine classes are grouped around a central space at the lower level leading directly onto the playground whilst the hall, administration and service accommodation are all on the upper level near to the car park and main entrance.

Internally the roof structure is exposed, with queen post trusses over the central area and hall, and purlins and rafters over cross walls elsewhere. Bands of glazing in the roof light the hall and the central space and the rear of classrooms.

The single sweeping multi-pitch roof is reminiscent of a circus marquee. The primitive decoration, including tiled zig-zag patterning, raised ridge board, and carved finials is intended to introduce an element of fairy tale. It should appeal to the imagination of a child, as well as being a source of visual excitement to the local community.

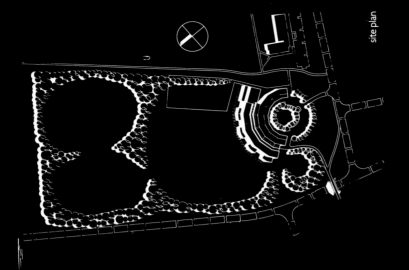

site plan

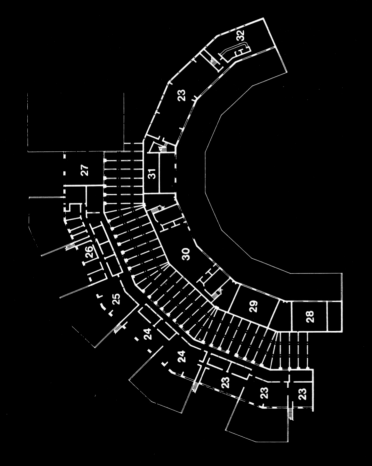

first floor plan

ground floor plan

CRESTWOOD SCHOOL AND COMMUNITY CENTRE

KEY

1.	SCIENCE	17.	TEXTILE DESIGN
2.	MATHS	18.	HOME ECONOMICS
3.	LANGUAGES	19.	DINING ROOM
4.	ENGLISH	20.	PLANT ROOM
5.	COMMERCE	21.	KITCHEN
6.	HISTORY	23.	SOCIAL
7.	GEOGRAPHY	24.	LIBRARY
8.	DRAMA	25.	STAFF ROOM
9.	GYMNASIUM	26.	ADMINISTRATION SUITE
10.	GIRLS CHANGING	27.	UPPER PART OF DRAMA
11.	BOYS CHANGING	28.	UPPER PART OF
12.	METALWORK		METALWORK
13.	WOODWORK	29.	UPPER PART OF
14.	TECHNICAL DRAWING		WOODWORK
15.	GENERAL ART	30.	MUSIC
16.	POTTERY	31.	TANKROOM
		32.	COMMUNITY BAR

CRESTWOOD SCHOOL

Crestwood is built on the edge of a level site near to a local shopping centre. The piazza formed between the shops and the school leads directly into a landscaped arcade with glazed roof and generous planting of trees which forms the main circulation area for the school. This arcade confers a number of benefits:

it provides excellent protected circulation space between the buildings and a substantial protected area for leisure on a site with a fairly hostile natural environment;

it lends itself readily to use as additional teaching areas for some subjects, at certain times of the year;

it offers significant advantages for energy conservation since some heat transfer from the school to the arcade is beneficial to conditions in the arcade and insulation provided from enclosing the arcade is beneficial to the school.

The arcade is used for activities as diverse as weddings and beer festivals and has become an established focal point for social activities. The community facilities provided as part of the school are directly related to the piazza, strengthening the link between school and local residents.

RINGWOOD SPORTS CENTRE

An existing conventional sports hall was extended in height and area to contain five badminton courts, as well as providing for basketball, five-a-side football etc. Four squash courts and a general activity room were provided at first floor level on top of existing changing accommodation which was left largely unaltered. Two of the courts have glass backs to enable viewing from a gallery at court level.

Swimming is catered for by a 25 metre, 5-lane, level-deck pool with a separate learner pool. Pool purification is by an ozone process and a heat pump transfers heat from the exhaust air to input air. The saving in energy achieved will pay for the pump after five years use. The pools with their new changing accommodation have been provided in an extension of the original building. This also contains a restaurant bar and viewing facilities over the top of the entrance hall, learner pool and wet changing rooms, with extensive views of the main pool and sports hall.

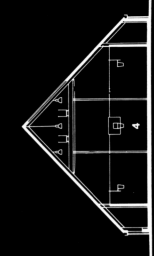

RINGWOOD SPORTS CENTRE

transverse section

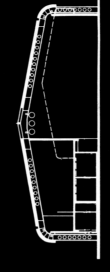

HENRY CORT SPORTS HALL

transverse section

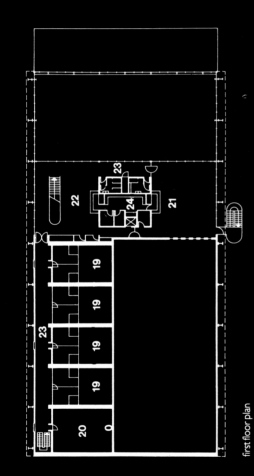

first floor plan

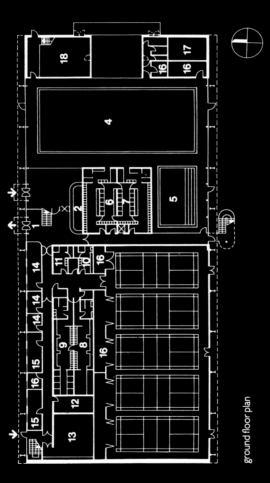

ground floor plan

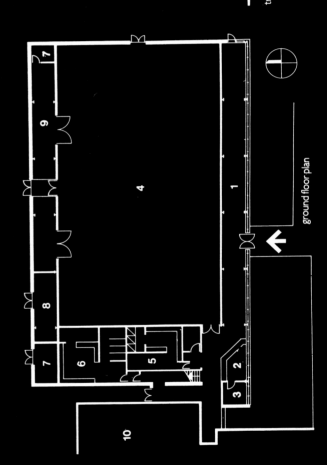

ground floor plan

The main structure comprises single portal frames spanning 30 metres with secondary support steel for the side walls. The roof is of profiled aluminium sheet with ridge roof-lighting and the curved eaves are manufactured from flat bonded aluminium sheet. Side walls at the pool end are of solar control glass in gasket glazed aluminium framing and, at the hall end, profiled steel sheeting with bonded insulation.

HENRY CORT SPORTS HALL

In recognition of the developing community role served by Henry Cort School and the need for additional indoor sporting facilities in the area, Fareham Borough Council and Hampshire County Council joined forces to finance the construction of a new sports hall to extend existing facilities and provide a focal point for community interests.

A fresh approach to the design of the hitherto traditional sports hall 'box' was adopted in an effort to reduce the costs normally associated with high walls and flat roofs. The portal 'A' frame structure supports a large pitched roof under which additional accommodation is provided at less than a proportionate increase in cost.

The design also aims to achieve a high level of daylight in the sports hall in order to create a light and spacious ambience. A translucent polyester sail cloth ceiling diffuses an expanse of north light glazing in the apex of the structural frame. Control of daylight in this way avoids the possibility of disabling glare, and also serves to protect the artificial lighting above the sail cloth which is similarly diffused.

The building contract was a fixed priced package deal based upon sketch plans and a performance specification, intended to take advantage of contractors' competitiveness and speed of performance in the design-and-construct field.

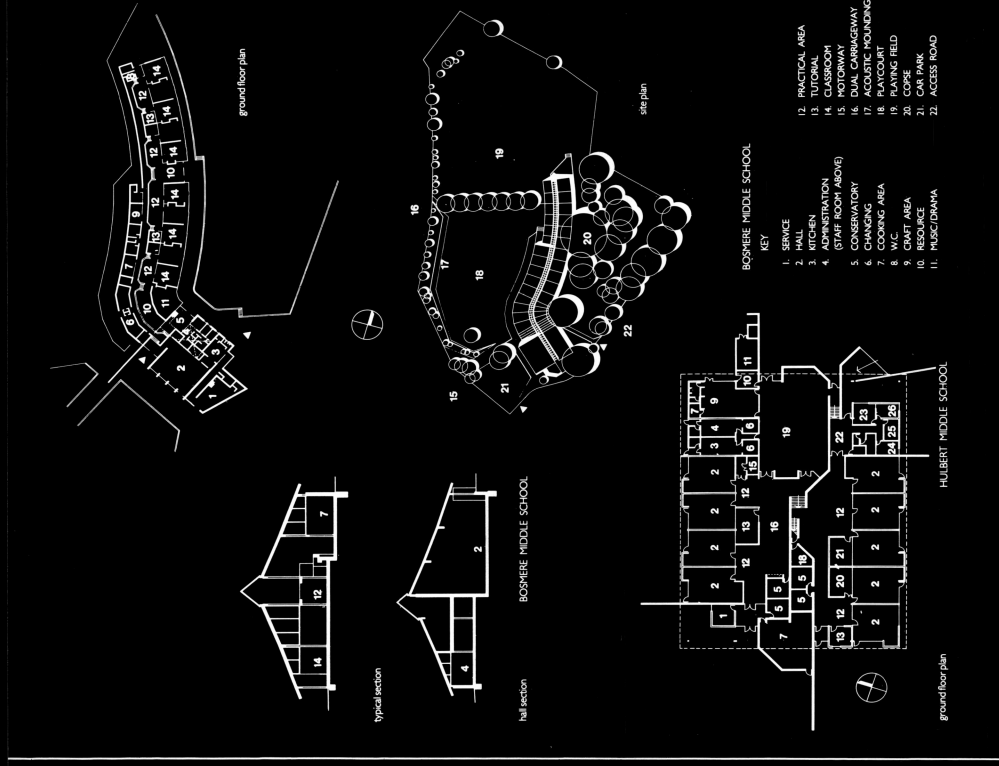

ground floor plan

site plan

BOSMERE MIDDLE SCHOOL

typical section

hall section

BOSMERE MIDDLE SCHOOL

HULBERT MIDDLE SCHOOL

ground floor plan

BOSMERE MIDDLE SCHOOL

KEY

1. SERVICE
2. HALL
3. KITCHEN
4. ADMINISTRATION (STAFF ROOM ABOVE)
5. CONSERVATORY
6. CHANGING
7. COOKING AREA
8. W.C.
9. CRAFT AREA
10. RESOURCE
11. MUSIC/DRAMA
12. PRACTICAL AREA
13. TUTORIAL
14. CLASSROOM
15. MOTORWAY
16. DUAL CARRAGEWAY
17. ACOUSTIC MOUNDING
18. PLAYCOURT
19. PLAYING FIELD
20. COPSE
21. CAR PARK
22. ACCESS ROAD

BOSMERE MIDDLE SCHOOL

Bosmere School lies in the north east angle between a new elevated motorway and a distributor road. The four acre site is softened by a dense copse to the east, containing a number of mature oaks. There were limited points for vehicular access, and it was necessary to maintain the operation of the existing school during the construction period. These factors led to the design of a single storey curvilinear building, winding its way among the trees, with a hard protective edge facing the roads. The anticipated traffic noise and pollution made a controlled internal environment essential.

The upper school is accommodated in a group of five classrooms with their related practical and resource areas separated from a similar lower school by a library area: all these spaces face onto the copse with direct access to outside teaching areas.

An entrance conservatory separates the teaching wings from the administrative areas, and allows a gradual transition from outside to inside to take place almost unnoticeably, by bringing landscaping into the heart of the building.

HULBERT MIDDLE SCHOOL

Hulbert School's ten acre site lies in the former grounds of a large house, demolished some years ago. A primary design aim was to preserve the many fine specimen trees and areas of fir copse.

The building itself incorporates changes of level, necessitated by the slope of the site, which delineate three areas of accommodation: an upper school for 10-12 year old pupils, a lower school for 8-10 year old pupils, and a central zone of two-storey staff and shared facilities. The whole of this accommodation is placed under one wide span pitched roof, clad in corrugated aluminium sheeting. This is supported by portal frames of hardwood, developed by the Timber Research and Development Association from their farm building systems.

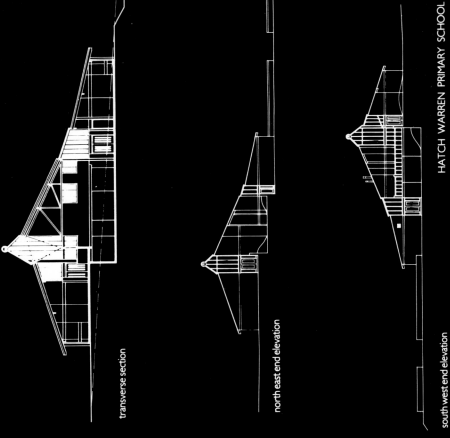

HULBERT MIDDLE SCHOOL

KEY

1. GROUP ROOM
2. CLASSROOM
3. GIRLS CHANGING
4. BOYS CHANGING
5. W.C.
6. SHOWERS
7. STORE
9. KITCHEN
10. CARETAKER
11. PLANT ROOM
12. PRACTICAL AREA
13. TUTORIAL ROOM
15. KILN ROOM
16. CENTRAL SPACE
17. MUSIC/DRAMA
18. CENTRAL STORE
19. HALL
20. CRAFTS AREA
21. COOKING AREA
22. RECEPTION
23. OFFICE
24. HEADMASTERS OFFICE
25. DEPUTY HEADMASTERS OFFICE
26. MEDICAL ROOM

HATCH WARREN PRIMARY SCHOOL

KEY

1. RECEPTION
2. HALL
3. CENTRAL AREA
4. CLASSROOM
5. TUTORIAL
6. MUSIC/DRAMA
7. KITCHEN
8. ADMINISTRATION

transverse section

north east end elevation

south west end elevation

HATCH WARREN PRIMARY SCHOOL

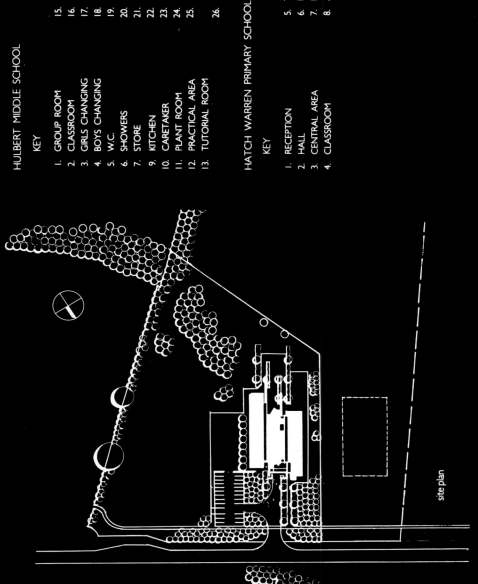

site plan

ground floor plan

Classrooms are divided by studwork partitions incorporating high level glazed screens. External walls are clad in cedar boarding on timber studs and glazed screens. In the central zone brick retaining walls penetrate the building from outside to support the first floor accommodation and define the changes of floor level.

The form of the building combines the benefits of a deep plan layout with the maximum use of daylighting and natural ventilation. Windows are concentrated on the south side of the building with roof overhangs to prevent summer overheating.

HATCH WARREN SCHOOL

The school is on a hillside on the western outskirts of Basingstoke serving new housing which in future years is planned to develop over the adjoining open fields. In this setting, the school is intended to project a striking and welcoming image.

The site is very exposed and the school is dug into the slope of the ground with existing tree belts extended up to each end of the building. The trees continue throughout the length of the inside of the building, along the upper corridor, as 'tree' shaped posts and trusses.

The building is on three tiers. Administration and infant classes are on the upper level. The hall is on the lower level in the centre of the school where there is most height, with the kitchen on the same level and staff room above. The junior classes are also on the lower level at the perimeter of the building, and a resource area and music/drama room is on an intermediate floor. The upper level cantilevers over the hall giving a viewing balcony.

Between the three tiers are two roof-glazed corridors with glazed screens in what otherwise are blank end facades. The three tiers are staggered diagonally across the length of the building affording articulation to the blank ends.

ELSON INFANT SCHOOL

This new building replaces the existing '40s concrete and timber hutted school.

Shared teaching areas and a sheltered courtyard are enclosed between the rectangular forms of the administration/hall/music/service blocks and a curvilinear class/base element, which opens up to the south via sliding glazed doors onto outside work spaces, playing field, and trees.

A low maintenance shell was provided through the use of highly insulated brickwork, and fibre cement/lead roof covering. Internally, a laminated timber post and beam frame gives spacial flexibility and, with glazed full height screens, a feeling of lightness and space, whilst continuous double glazed roof lighting provides generous daylight. Manually controlled roof and wall vents give a wide range of ventilation control for all seasonal conditions.

Re-use of the existing road, parking, playcourts, and playing fields enabled an area 15% above the Department of Education and Science minimum to be achieved within cost limits whilst incorporating a high specification of materials, finishes and landscaping.

BURNHAM COPSE SCHOOL

The Burnham Copse School site is within a badly run-down area and an important objective of the design was to provide a strong visual focal point in its redevelopment.

The building develops the theme of Four Lanes Primary School Chineham and consists of a classroom block and a hall block connected by a small glazed link.

To demonstrate that every class forms an integral part of the whole school (a firmly held philosophical tenet amongst local education advisers) all the classrooms are given equal importance by placing them around a central shared area, thus preventing any sense of visual isolation. This arrangement gives each classroom ample external glazing and allows for a separate well-lit class base alongside.

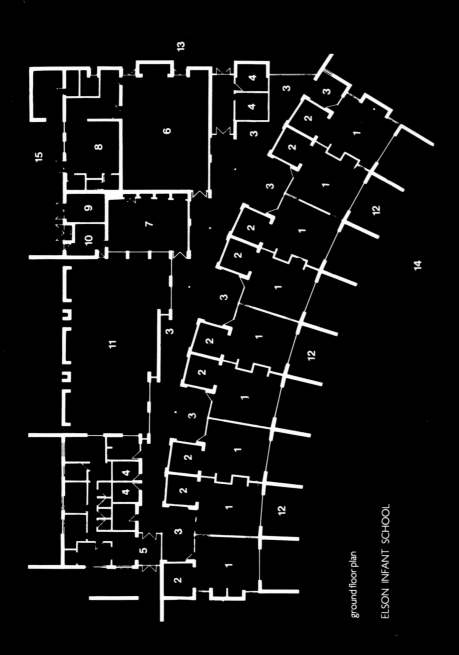

ground floor plan

ELSON INFANT SCHOOL

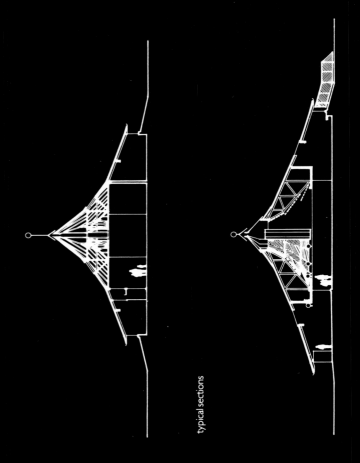

typical sections

ELSON INFANT SCHOOL

KEY

1. CLASSROOM
2. HOME BASE
3. SHARED/RESOURCE AREA
4. W.C.
5. ENTRANCE HALL
6. HALL
7. MUSIC/DRAMA
8. KITCHEN
9. PLANT ROOM
10. CARETAKER
11. COURTYARD
12. OUTSIDE WORKING
13. PLAYCOURT
14. PLAYING FIELD
15. SERVICE

BURNHAM COPSE INFANT SCHOOL

KEY

1. NEW SCHOOL
2. PLAYGROUND
3. SOFT PLAY AREA
4. SERVICE YARD
5. PARKING

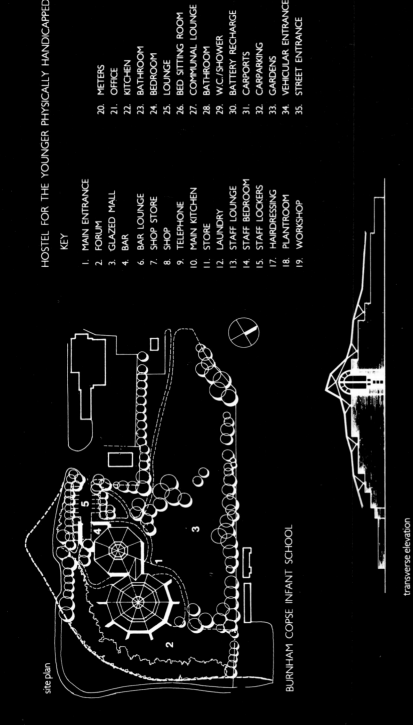

KEY

1. MAIN ENTRANCE
2. FORUM
3. GLAZED MALL
4. BAR
6. BAR LOUNGE
7. SHOP STORE
8. SHOP
9. TELEPHONE
10. MAIN KITCHEN
11. STORE
12. LAUNDRY
13. STAFF LOUNGE
14. STAFF BEDROOM
15. STAFF LOCKERS
17. HAIRDRESSING
18. PLANTROOM
19. WORKSHOP
20. METERS
21. OFFICE
22. KITCHEN
23. BATHROOM
24. BEDROOM
25. LOUNGE
26. BED SITTING ROOM
27. COMMUNAL LOUNGE
28. BATHROOM
29. W.C./SHOWER
30. BATTERY RECHARGE
31. CARPORTS
32. CARPARKING
33. GARDENS
34. VEHICULAR ENTRANCE
35. STREET ENTRANCE

site plan

BURNHAM COPSE INFANT SCHOOL

transverse elevation

longitudinal elevation

ground floor plan

HOSTEL FOR THE YOUNGER PHYSICALLY HANDICAPPED

The administration and service rooms are grouped around the hall, in the second block, with the main entrances, both for visitors and pupils, located through the link.

The tent-like, multi-pitch roof shapes of glass, slate and tiles arranged in decorative patterns are intended to stimulate the imagination of small children and, with the unusual shapes and bright colours within, produce an environment which may well linger in their memories.

HOSTEL FOR THE YOUNGER PHYSICALLY HANDICAPPED

The building design emphasises the functional importance of privacy in the 24 residents' bedsitting rooms. These are of generous size and are arranged in five irregular groups of four to six rooms along the east side of a central arcade. The rooms in each group open onto semi-private shared spaces which are used for dining and other group activities.

A large communal room, or 'forum', is available for formal and informal use by residents, including those in six sheltered living units, provided on the west side of the arcade for less severely disabled people.

The building has a strong spinal form, with the shallow pitched roof rising to a glazed ridge over a central arcade. Frequent changes of axis and width prevent any monotony within the arcade, which is given an outdoor flavour by the finishing materials used and extensive planting. Precautions are taken against excessive heat gain in summer by permanent ventilation at the gables, eaves and ridge.

The roof acts as a shield from rain and wind and admits light to the centre of a deep plan building. Heat and sound insulation are provided by a sub roof over the cellular accommodation beneath the main umbrella. The roof structure is a light steel frame with aluminium and PVC covering and the rooms below are of traditional brick and timber construction.

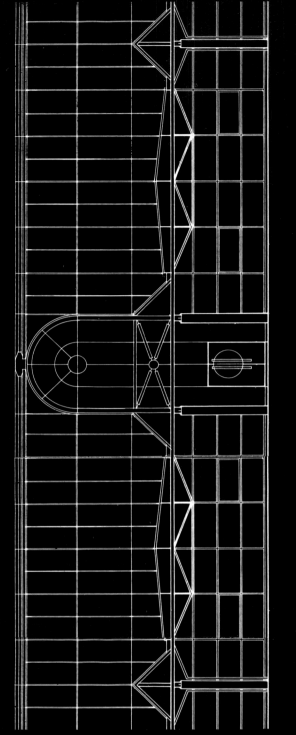

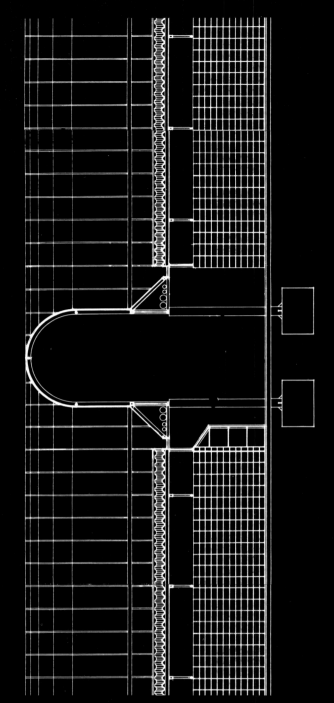

part elevation

part section

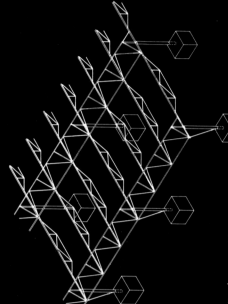

structural axonometric

FARNBOROUGH COLLEGE OF TECHNOLOGY

The design is a response to the particular problems of the College and the financial strategy for its redevelopment. Its objectives were:

to unite both existing and new accommodation to form a coherent overall development;

to provide accommodation capable of meeting changing requirements during the design period and following occupation;

to provide a design of architectural and environmental quality which established a dynamic image suited to the changing role of such a college in the 1980s.

The construction is based on prefabricated components, which can be varied according to detailed requirements without affecting the overall building structure and its envelope. A single storey steel frame is located on a repetitive grid. This is integrated with an overhead services grid and roof glazing to give natural lighting to deep-plan areas.

An overall planning strategy was developed for the whole site which involved the zoning of facilities. Car parking and service access is provided on the north side of the site with adjoining communal facilities such as the library, lecture theatre and refectory.

The teaching facilities of individual departments are positioned to the south of this around landscaped courtyards. Within this area there is a similar zoning of highly serviced areas, such as laboratories, and general teaching space. This planning and servicing matrix can accommodate a high degree of change.

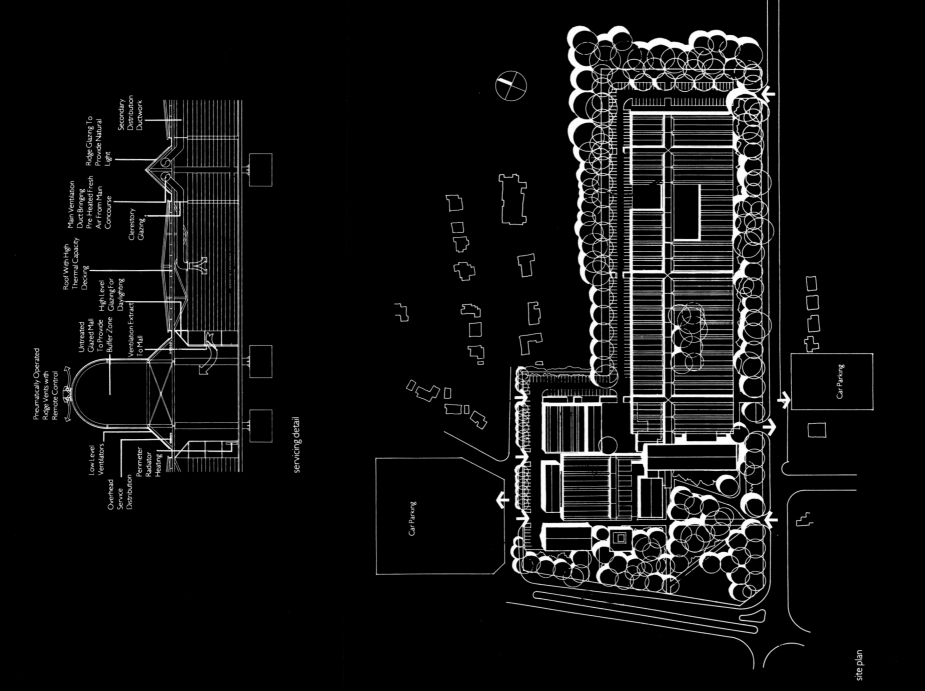

servicing detail

Pneumatically Operated
Ridge Vents with
Remote Control

Low Level
Ventilators

Overhead
Service
Distribution

Perimeter
Radiator
Heating

Untreated
Glazed Mall
To Provide
Buffer Zone

Ventilation Extract
To Mall

Roof With High
Thermal Capacity
Decking

High Level
Glazing For
Daylighting

Main Ventilation
Duct Bringing
Pre-Heated Fresh
Air From Main
Concourse

Clerestory
Glazing

Ridge Glazing To
Provide Natural
Light

Secondary
Distribution
Ductwork

site plan

Car Parking

Car Parking

Important elements of the design are the glazed streets which form links between departments. These spaces are unheated but give protection from rain and wind, and are developments from previous projects such as the conservatory at Newlands Primary School, Yateley.

The glazed malls also act as buffer zones to reduce noise intrusion and heating requirements for adjacent spaces. Solar gains are employed to pre-heat ventilation losses.

There is a strong design similarity in the use of such malls with recent shopping developments. This was a conscious decision to encourage greater public and commercial use of the college facilities, and avoid the institutional character of many similar educational establishments.

This planning strategy would allow for alternative commercial usage of certain zones should this become desirable in the event of falling student numbers.

HAMPSHIRE COUNTY ARCHITECTS

Scheme	Date	Design Team	Interior Designer	Landscape Designer	Quantity Surveyor
Fort Hill Community School Basingstoke	1978	Trevor Harris John Laye Peter Galloway	——	Stephen Harte	Cyril Sweett and Partners
St. Francis Special School Fareham	1978	David White Alistair Macdonald	——	——	John Duggan
River Hamble Harbourmaster's Office Warsash	1978	Michael Morris	——	——	Keith Bailey
Newlands Primary School Yateley	1979	Mervyn Perkins	——	Ken Johnson Trevor Goodenough	Langdon and Every
Library Chandlers Ford	1981	Colin Stansfield Smith Barry Bryant	Terry Riggs	Ken Johnson	John Duggan Gordon Legg
Rookwood Infant School Eastleigh	1981	Neill Beasley Jon Dale	——	Ken Johnson	Don Eatwell
Four Lanes Primary School Chineham	1982	Ian Templeton Stephen Harte	Terry Riggs	Stephen Harte	Paul Stuart
Crestwood School and Community Centre Eastleigh	1982	Huw Thomas David White Alistair MacDonald	——	Pirkko Higson and Associates	Dearle and Henderson
Henry Cort School Sports Hall Fareham	1982	Neill Beasley David Smith	——	——	John Wickers
Ringwood Sports Centre Ringwood	1982	David White Norman Roberts Alec Upton	——	——	Davis Belfield and Everest
Hulbert Middle School Waterlooville	1982	Mervyn Perkins David White John Godding	——	——	Davis Belfield and Everest
Bosmere Middle School Havant	1983	Neville Churcher Peter Galloway Mervyn Perkins	——	Ken Johnson	John Smith Associates
Hatch Warren Primary School Basingstoke	1984	Stephen Harte	Terry Riggs	Stephen Harte	Kenneth Marsh and Partners
Elson Infant School Gosport	1984	Neville Churcher Alec Upton	——	Trevor Goodenough	Dadson and Butler (Gosport)
Hostel for the Younger Physically Handicapped Eastleigh	1985	David White Alistair MacDonald Alec Upton	David Morriss	Pirkko Higson and Associates	Dearle and Henderson
Burnham Copse Infant School Tadley	1985	Ian Templeton Ian Lower	——	Christianne Strubbe (County Planning Department)	Langdon and Every
Farnborough College of Technology Farnborough	1986	Mervyn Perkins Peter Galloway John Godding Kevin Harnett Peter Hayne Mark Ogden	Duffy, Eley, Giffone and Worthington	Jakobsen Landscape Architects	Dearle and Henderson

ARCHITECTURAL CONSULTANTS

Portsmouth Polytechnic Library Portsmouth	1979	AHRENDS, BURTON AND KORALEK P. Koralek J. Watson	——	Michael Brown Landscape Architects	Monk Dunstone Associates
Calthorpe Park Secondary School Refurbishment Fleet	1984	EDWARD CULLINAN ARCHITECTS E. Cullinan T. Peake A. Short G. Pendyre	——	Edward Cullinan Architects/Ken Johnson	Willis and Thompson
Library and Health Centre Portchester	1984	JACKSON, GREENEN, DOWN AND PARTNERS N. Beasley	——	Lisney Associates	Alistair MacDonald
D-Day Museum Portsmouth	1984	PORTSMOUTH CITY ARCHITECT'S DEPARTMENT K. V. Norrish M. Gill M. Tozer	Portsmouth City Architect's Department: K. V. Norrish J. Sparkes	Portsmouth City Architect's Department: K. V. Norrish J. Wigham	Monk Dunstone Associates
Southampton Hall of Aviation Southampton	1984	SOUTHAMPTON CITY ARCHITECT'S DEPARTMENT J. Neyroud P. Hoadley R. Benn	——	G. Pocock (City Planning Department)	Langdon and Every
Special School and Hostel Project Basingstoke	1985	ALDINGTON, CRAIG & COLLINGE P. Collinge R. Partridge P. Clark	——	——	Langdon and Every
Library Bordon	1985	EVANS, ROBERTS AND PARTNERS R. Adam			Bob Price

Structural Engineer	Mechanical Engineer	Electrical Engineer	Clerk of Works	General Contractor
Arup Associates	Arup Associates	Arup Associates	Maurice Smith	Goodall, Barnard and Clayton Ltd.
Roger Goodier	Arup Associates	Arup Associates	Ernest Tucker	Louis Thompson (Southern) Ltd.
D. J. Doughty Associates Ltd. (Civil Engineer)	——	——	Peter Simpson	Tilbury Construction Ltd.
Anthony Hunt Associates	Adams Green and Partners	Roy Yeoman	Brian Carrier	H. N. Edwards and Partners Ltd.
Anthony Hunt Associates	Fuller and Partners	Fuller and Partners	Peter Simpson	Brazier and Son Ltd.
D. H. Robinson Associates	D. R. Chick and Partners	Simon Tribe	Bill Bamber	Louis Thompson (Southern) Ltd.
Brian Veck	Chris Staple	Roy Yeoman	Dennis Holloway	H. N. Edwards and Partners Ltd.
Anthony Hunt Associates	Steenson Varming Mulcahy	Steenson Varming Mulcahy	John Cowie	Bryan Vear Builders Ltd.
Anthony Ward and Partners (Alresford)	Brian Evans	Bruce McDermott	Terry Pitt	Hill Industrial Ltd
Anthony Hunt Associates Dale and Goldfinger	Dale and Goldfinger Anthony Hunt Associates	Roy Yeoman	Brian Carrier	Wiltshier Construction Ltd
Timber Research and Development Association	Marchant Filer Dixon	Jim Alesbury	Geoffrey Stevenson	John Worman Ltd.
Roger Goodier	Fuller and Partners	Roy Yeoman	Geoffrey Stevenson	Henry Jones and Son (Portsmouth) Ltd.
Barron and Partners	King Cathery Partnership	Roy Yeoman	Dennis Holloway	H. N. Edwards and Partners Ltd.
D. H. Robinson Associates	Chris Staple	Simon Tribe	Terry Pitt	Barnes and Elliott (Portsmouth) Ltd.
Malcolm Gates	Alan Dowdell	Bruce McDermott	John Cowie	George and Harding Ltd.
Brian Veck Malcolm Gates	David Wright Derek Yeomans	Roy Yeoman	Dennis Holloway	W. M. Annette and Co. Ltd.
Anthony Hunt Associates	Dale and Goldfinger	Dale and Goldfinger	Malcolm Ross	Kyle Steward Ltd.
Arup Associates	Zisman Bowyer and Partners	Zisman Bowyer and Partners	R. E. Foster Partners	W. E. Chivers and Son
S. Jampel and Partners	Max Fordham and Partners	——	J. Preston	H. N. Edwards and Partners Ltd.
Thompson Barnfather and Partners	Chris Staple	Simon Tribe	Geoffrey Stevenson	Louis Thompson (Southern) Ltd.
Portsmouth City Engineer's Department	IEI	IEI	J. Crew	Waring (Contractors) Ltd.
P. Gregory (City Engineer's and Surveyor's Department)	Southampton City Architect's Department: B. Dannan	Southampton City Architect's Department: D. Thick	R. Bezzant	Brims and Co. Ltd.
Anthony Hunt Associates	King Cathery Partnership	King Cathery Partnership	——	——
Scott White and Hookins	Peter Collings	Jim Alesbury	——	Jenkins and Sons Ltd.
Scott White and Hookins	Price Grant Associates	Price Grant Associates	——	——
Buro Happold	Buro Happold	Buro Happold	——	——

SPONSORSHIP

The publication of this book has been sponsored by members of the architectural and building community and the authors would like to thank the following for their support:

REDLAND BRICKS LIMITED and REDLAND ROOF TILES LIMITED

who have given a substantial and generous proportion of the total costs

also:

Adams Green & Partners
building services engineers

Ahrends Burton & Koralek
architects

Aldington Craig & Collinge
architects

Arc Concrete Ltd (Arc Conbloc)

Ove Arup Partnership
engineers

Baker & Martin
structural engineers

Barron & Partners
structural engineers

Bartlett Gilbert & Co Ltd
building contractors

Brazier & Son Ltd
building contractors

Peter Brett Associates
structural engineers

Brims & Co Ltd
building & engineering contractors

A. Buckett & Son Ltd
electrical & heating contractors

Burt Boulton (Timber) Ltd

Carron Heating Ltd

D. R. Chick & Partners
building services engineers

Dadson & Butler
quantity surveyors

Dale & Goldfinger
building services engineers

Davis Belfield & Everest
quantity surveyors

A. Dean (Farnham) Ltd
heating & ventilating contractors

Dearle & Henderson
quantity surveyors

Drake & Scull Engineering Ltd
mechanical & electrical contractors

H. N. Edwards & Partners Ltd
building contractors

Evans Roberts & Partners
architects & town planners

Ferguson & Partners
building services engineers

Fuller & Partners
building services engineers

George & Harding Ltd
builders & joinery manufacturers

Goodall Barnard Ltd
building contractors

Harding McDermott & Partners
mechanical & electrical contractors

Harris & Sutherland
civil & structural engineers

Pirkko Higson, Ken Jones, Stuart Pearson
landscape architects

Hill Industrial Ltd
building contractors

Hoburne Development Co Ltd
building contractors

Michael Hopkins Architects

Houghton Greenlees & Associates
structural and building services engineers

Anthony Hunt Associates
structural engineers

Jackson Greenen Down & Partners
architects & town planners

King Cathery Partnership
building services engineers

Langdon & Every
quantity surveyors

Marchant Filer Dixon
structural and building services engineers

Marley PLC

Kenneth Marsh & Partners
quantity surveyors

Portsmouth City Council
architects department

W. E. Preston Ltd
building and engineering contractors

D. H. Robinson Associates
structural engineers

Sherlow Electrical Contractors Ltd

John Smith Associates
quantity surveyors

Solaglas Mackenzie Ltd

Southampton City Council
architects department

Steensen Varming Mulcahy & Partners
building services engineers

Structural Timbers Ltd

Cyril Sweett & Partners
quantity surveyors

Test Valley Engineers Ltd

Louis Thompson (Southern) Ltd
building contractors

Thompson Barnfather & Partners
structural engineers

Tilbury Construction Ltd
building contractors

Bryan Vear Builders Ltd

R. F. Webb Ltd
electrical contractors

Wilson Large & Partners
quantity surveyors

PHOTOGRAPHY

Ahrends Burton & Koralek, p. 55

Aldington Craig & Collinge, p. 58-59

Architects' Journal, p. 54

Architects' Journal/Richard Bryant, p. 35

Richard Bryant, p. 4-6, 32-33, 38-39, 67-69, inside back cover

Edward Cullinan Architects/Martin Charles, p. 60-61

Evans Roberts & Partners/Robert Adam, p. 64-65

Geg Germany, p. 42-45, 70-71

Hampshire County Council, p. 2, 8-11, 13-16, 18-21, 25, 30-31, 36, 37, 40-41, 72, 76-77, 79-93

Michael Hopkins Architects, p. 62-63

Jackson Greenen Down & Partners, p. 52-53

Joe Low, p. 56

Christine Ottewill, p. 22-24, 50-51, 74-75

Jo Reid and John Peck/H.C.C., p. 26-29, 46-49

Transplastix Ltd/Hemingway Incorporated Photographers, p. 57

PRODUCTION

David White

David J. Morriss

Geoffrey Burnaby   Editor

Alison Garland   Studio
John Woodhead

Newlands Primary School
Yateley
1979

BIBLIOGRAPHY

AC (SWITZERLAND)

Vol. 28, No. 1(107), 1983
Newlands Primary School, Yateley

ARCHITECTS JOURNAL

Vol. 168, No. 51/52, December 1978
St Francis Special School, Fareham

Vol. 170, No. 48, November 1979
Harbourmaster's Office, Warsash

Vol. 171, Nos. 11 & 13, March 1980
'The Educating Style'
Fort Hill Secondary School, Basingstoke

Vol. 171, No. 16, April 1980
'Public Panache'
Six HCC projects

Vol. 173, No. 13, April 1981
Ringwood Sports Centre

Vol. 173, No. 25, June 1981
Newlands Primary School, Yateley

Vol. 176, No. 42, October 1982
Fareham and Ringwood Sports Centres

Vol. 178, No. 33, August 1983
Chandlers Ford Library

Vol. 180, No. 50, December 1984
'Trio in Pitch': Four Lanes Primary,
Hulbert Middle, Bosmere Middle School

ARCHITECTURAL DESIGN

No. 3/4, 1984
Burnham Copse Infant School, Tadley

ARCHITECTURAL REVIEW

Vol. 167, No. 995, January 1980
Newlands Primary School, Yateley

Vol. 171, No. 1019, January 1982
Preview 1982: Chandler's Ford Library
and Four Lanes Primary School, Chineham

Vol. 172, No. 1025, July 1982
Crestwood Secondary School & Rookwood Primary School

Vol. 178, No. 1056, January 1985
Calthorpe Park Secondary School

Vol. 178, No. 1058, April 1985
Elson Infant School, Gosport
Bosmere Middle School, Havant

BAUMEISTER

Vol. 179, May 1982
Fort Hill Secondary School, Basingstoke

BUILDING DESIGN

No. 446, May 1979
Fort Hill Secondary School, Basingstoke

No. 663, September 1981
'Councils can be Creative'

No. 605, August 1983
Ringwood Sports Centre

CIBS JOURNAL

Vol. 6, No. 12, December 1984
'Small is Beautiful'
Newlands Primary School, Yateley

CONCRETE QUARTERLY

No. 133, April/June 1982
Fort Hill Secondary School, Basingstoke

DEUTSCHE BAUZEITUNG

Vol. 117, No. 8, August 1983
Crestwood Secondary School, Eastleigh

DOMUS

No. 637, March 1983
Newlands Primary School, Yateley

ENERGY IN BUILDINGS

Vol. 1, No. 1, October 1982
Hulbert Middle School, Waterlooville

LANDSCAPE DESIGN

No. 133, February 1981
Fort Hill Secondary School, Basingstoke

RIBA JOURNAL

Vol. 88, No. 3, March 1981
Crestwood Secondary School
Portsmouth Polytechnic: Saving Energy
Wellow Primary School

Vol. 88, No. 8, August 1981
St Francis Special School, Fareham

Vol. 89, No. 8, August 1982
Fort Hill Secondary School, Basingstoke

Vol. 90, No. 8, August 1983
Newlands Primary School, Yateley

RIBA 'TRANSACTIONS 6'

Vol. 3, No. 2, 1984
'Developments in Social Architecture in Hampshire'
RIBA lecture by Colin Stansfield Smith